Leadership Skills
High School Workbook

Leadership Skills
High School Workbook

Copyright © 2022 The Leadership Program

All rights reserved.

No part of this book may be reproduced, or stored in a retrieval system, or transmitted in any form or by any means, electronic, mechanical, photocopying, recording, or otherwise, without express written permission of the publisher.

Created by The Leadership Program, New York
www.theleadershipprogram.com

Leadership Skills—HS—VPP

The Leadership Program
535 8th Avenue, Floor 16
New York, NY 10018

Published by Girl Friday Books™, Seattle
www.girlfridaybooks.com

Produced by Girl Friday Productions

ISBN: 978-1-954854-81-9

Printed in the United States of America

Your Personal Companion

This is your place to record, draw, capture, digest, list, and absorb your leadership journey. In this companion you will encounter:

WORKSHEETS AND HANDOUTS

These are the information and activity pages that are part of each lesson.

QUESTIONS

These are questions with an emphasis on "quest." A *Question* offers you a chance to go further into what happened in class.

DIG INS

A Dig In is an opportunity for you to go to the next level in your personal leadership journey.

Contents

1. INTRODUCTION TO LEADERSHIP
Introduction to Leadership
- Brainstorming Process Ground Rules 2
- My Leadership 3
- How Was Brainstorming? 4

Leadership Password
- Real-Life Leaders 5
- What Qualities Do You Remember? 6

Setting Expectations
- Setting S.M.A.R.T. Goals 7
- Leadership Contract 9
- Goal Grid 10

2. SELF-CONCEPT
Guess Who I Am
- A "Me" Inventory 12
- Name Drawing 13
- *Questions* 14

Your Many Roles
- Your Many Roles 15
- Role Analysis 16
- *Questions* 17

My Interests
- Statement of Interest 18

Great Plates
- "I Bring..." Drawing 19

Guess Who Said It
- *Questions* 20

3. GROUP DYNAMICS
Human Barometer
- Your P.O.V. 22

Machines
- Machine Checklist 23
- Work with Me 24

Labels
- *Questions* 25
- Dig In 26

Diversity Pursuit
- Diversity Pursuit 27
- *Questions* 28

1, 2, 3, Video!
- *Questions* 29
- Dig In 30

Paper Clip Chain Game
- Paper Clip Chain Directions 31
- *Questions* 32
- Dig In 33

Detective Leader
- *Questions* 34
- Dig In 35

4 VISION AND IMAGINATION

Biography of a Stranger: Part 1
- Biography of a Stranger 38
- Three Lines and a Secret 39

Biography of a Stranger: Part 2
- Dig Deeper 40

Steppin' Up
- Steppin' Up Rules 41
- Steppin' Up My Future 42

Goals, Plan, Action!
- Your Plan of Action 43
- Tribute to You 44

5 CONFLICT MANAGEMENT

Role Play
- Role Play Setup 46
- Dialogue Writing 47
- *Questions* 48
- Dig In 49

Conflict Scramble
- Conflict Detective 50
- *Questions* 51
- Dig In 52

Active Listening: Introduction
- Are You an Effective Communicator? 53
- Active Listening Vocabulary 54
- Are You Listening? 55
- *Questions* 56
- Dig In 57

Active Listening: Practice
- Active Listening Monologue 58
- Are You Really Listening? 60

"I" Messages
- Translation Sheet 61
- "I" Messages in Real Life 63

ABCs of Anger
- Responses to Anger 64
- Learning the ABCs of Anger 66
- The ABCs of Anger Worksheet 67
- Take My Advice 68
- Dig In 69

Givin' It
- Role Play Setup 70
- Givin' It Checklist 71
- Dialogue Writing 72
- *Questions* 73
- Dig In 74

Takin' It
- Role Play Setup 75
- Takin' It Checklist 76
- Dialogue Writing 77
- Dig In 78

Choices, Decisions, Consequences: Part 1
- To Blank or Not to Blank 79
- C.D.C.—Setting the Scene 80
- *Questions* 81

Choices, Decisions, Consequences: Part 2
- Choices, Decisions, Consequences Role Play 82
- Decisions 84

Dramas and Dilemmas
- *Questions* 85
- Dig In 86

Conflict and Me
- Conflict Management 87
- Conflict Statues 88

6 SOCIAL RESPONSIBILITY

Visions and Inventions
- *Questions* 90

Island Survivors
- Action Plan 91
- Action Plan Example 93
- Tribe Survival Mission 95
- Tiger Island Map 98
- Organizational Model 100
- *Questions* 101
- Dig In 102

7 PROJECT WORK

Who Am I?
- Who Am I? Project Guide 104
- *Questions* 107
- Dig In 108

Celebrating Who We Are
- Who Am I? Reflection 109
- Dig In 110

1
Introduction to Leadership

BRAINSTORMING PROCESS GROUND RULES

- Record all ideas.

- Make no critical judgments.

- Encourage freethinking. In other words: the wilder the idea, the better.

- Focus on quality, not quantity.

- Collaborate and expand upon others' ideas.

USE YOUR IMAGINATION!

NAME: _____

MY LEAVERSHIP

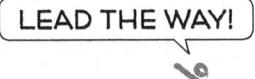  

WHAT LEADERSHIP QUALITIES DO YOU POSSESS?	WHERE IN YOUR LIFE CAN YOU USE THESE LEADERSHIP QUALITIES?
WHAT LEADERSHIP QUALITIES DO YOU WISH YOU HAD BUT FEEL YOU STRUGGLE WITH RIGHT NOW?	WHERE OR WHEN IN YOUR LIFE DO YOU FIND IT HARD TO EXHIBIT LEADERSHIP QUALITIES?

NAME:

HOW WAS BRAINSTORMING?

NAME: _____

REAL-LIFE LEADERS

 YOU LOOK UP TO...

I, ... , consider
.... to be a leader
in my life because ....
....
....
....
....
....
....
....
....
....
....
....
....
....
....
....
....

NAME: _____

WHAT QUALITIES DO YOU REMEMBER?

WHAT QUALITIES DO YOU REMEMBER FROM THE CLASS BRAINSTORM TODAY? WRITE THEM BELOW. NEXT TO EACH QUALITY, WRITE THE NAME OF SOMEONE YOU KNOW WHO EMBODIES THAT QUALITY.

QUALITY	PERSON

SETTING S.M.A.R.T. GOALS

Long-range goals point you in the right direction to achieve what really matters most in your life. Example: "I want to graduate from high school with honors."

Intermediate goals show you how to do it. Intermediate goals are easier to reach if you break them down into smaller steps. Example: "I need to get a B average this semester in my English class in order to achieve my long-range goal." You will reach these goals when they become part of your daily tasks.

Daily tasks tell you what you have to do today to achieve your long-range and intermediate goals. Example: "I need to read my English assignment for three hours today, from 5:00 p.m. to 8:00 p.m."

When you begin to set goals, be sure that they are S.M.A.R.T. goals:

Specific: An unwritten goal is merely a wish. Writing down the goal forces you to be specific. State exactly what you plan to accomplish. If a goal is not specific, you will have a hard time knowing whether or not you've reached it.

Measurable: You can see improvement only by measuring change. If you set a goal that can't be easily measured, such as "Be more honest," chances are you won't make much improvement.

Action-oriented: Set up things to be done. Goals should always focus on actions rather than personal qualities. Instead of having the goal "I will do my homework every day," write about specific actions. Example: "I will complete my homework every day from 4:00 p.m. to 5:30 p.m. at the desk in my room."

Realistic: Goals must be realistic. It's good to aim high, but if you aim too high, you might become discouraged, and the goal-setting process can become just another fruitless activity. On the other hand, goals that are too easily reached are just as useless as goals that are too far beyond your reach.

Timely: Be sure that you allow a reasonable amount of time. Don't set a goal for which you honestly don't have the time. Likewise, don't give yourself so much time that the goal becomes meaningless.

NAME: _____

LEADERSHIP CONTRACT

I, ..., as a member of The Leadership Program, agree to achieve the following **class** goals:

....
....
....
....
....
....
....

As an individual, I agree to achieve the following **personal** goal(s):

....
....
....
....
....
....
....

Signed: ....
Witness: ....

Witness: Each member of the class must choose a witness to his/her contract. Choose your witness carefully. The witness is a person who agrees to support you throughout the sessions. The witness congratulates you when you take steps toward the achievement of the goal. If you are having difficulty achieving the goal, the witness listens to you, provides support, and reviews modifications to the goal.

NAME: _____

GOAL GRID

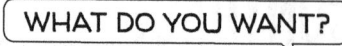 WHAT DO YOU WANT?

CATEGORY	MOST DIFFICULT TO ACHIEVE OR FOLLOW	IDEAS ON HOW TO BE SUCCESSFUL
GROUND RULE		
CLASS GOAL		
PERSONAL GOAL		

The Leadership Program

2
Self-Concept

NAME: _____

A "ME" INVENTORY

Three things I do extremely well:	Three things I do okay:	Three things I do, but I would be extremely happy never to do again:
Three things about myself that I really like:	Three things about myself that are okay:	Three things about myself that I wish I could change:
Three things other people think are good about me:	Three things that other people think are okay about me:	Three things that I wish other people didn't think about me:

After filling out the grid, draw a star next to all of the items that you can control. Example: I'm a good friend. Then draw a circle next to all the items you can't control. Example: I like my eyes.

NAME:

NAME DRAWING

Draw or attach your name drawing from class here.

NAME: _____

QUESTIONS

WHAT DO YOU THINK?

1. What was it like to share the story of your name?

2. What were the five positive things you wrote about yourself for the Guess Who I Am activity?

3. What are five more positive things about you that you didn't share?

NAME:

YOUR MANY ROLES

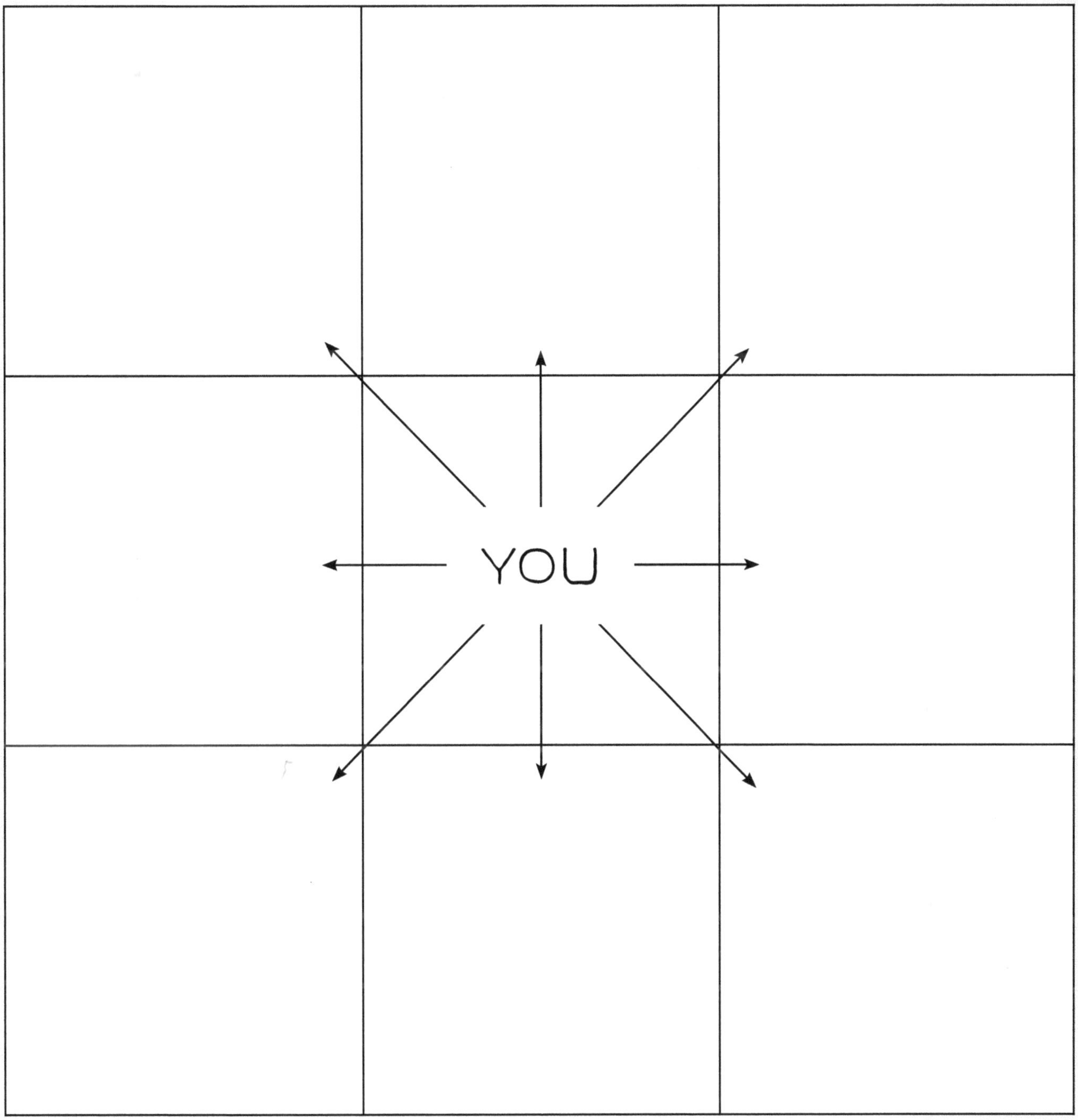

YOU

WOW! YOU'RE SO VERSATILE!

NAME:

ROLE ANALYSIS

Role #1:

Description:

Role #2:

Description:

Role #3:

Description:

NAME: _____

QUESTIONS

WHAT DO YOU THINK?

1. How did it feel to rate your performance in each role?

2. Is there anything you would like to change about your performance in any of your roles?

3. If so, what?

4. Who are the people who have roles in your life, and what are those roles?

NAME:

STATEMENT OF INTEREST

Review the interests you placed in each category. Think for a moment about what these interests might say about who you are. Write your conclusions in the space provided below.

NAME:

"I BRING..." DRAWING

Attach your "I Bring..." drawing here or make a drawing of the class "I Bring..." Collage.

NAME:

QUESTIONS

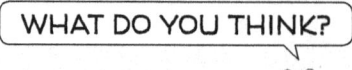

1. When you think about appreciation, what comes to mind?

2. Why is it important to know your positive qualities?

3. Is it okay to talk about your positive qualities? Why?

3
Group Dynamics

NAME:

YOUR P.O.V.

We disagreed with the other group(s) on the following question:

Two reasons that my group had a different point of view:

Reason 1:

GOOD POINT! I CAN SEE IT BOTH WAYS!

Reason 2:

What is a Human Barometer question that you would like the class to be asked? Why?

NAME: _____

MACHINE CHECKLIST

Directions:

1. Decide what kind of machine your group will create. Examples: a hair-washing machine, a laughter-producing machine, a fruit picking and processing machine, a shoe repair machine, etcetera.

2. Pick a representative from your group to go through the checklist to make sure that you've completed all of the requirements.

3. Let the teacher know when you are ready to share with the class.

Check each box when the task or element is complete:

❏ Every person in your group has participated in the function of the machine.

❏ Your machine has at least three moving parts.

❏ Your machine has at least three sounds.

❏ Your group has tested your machine before demonstrating it for the class.

❏ Your group has chosen a name for your machine.

Our machine is called:

NAME: _____

WORK WITH ME

Think of one project or activity that you have done that involved working with other people.

What was the project?

List the tasks or jobs that were needed for the project to succeed:

How did cooperation and teamwork benefit the overall result of the project?

Describe a project you would love to be part of in the future:

NAME:

QUESTIONS

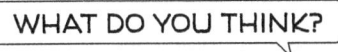

1. What are some labels people use for one another in your school?

2. What part do you play in labeling people?

3. How did you feel when you shared something positive about your classmates?

4. How did you feel about what your classmates said about you?

NAME:

DIG IN

Why is it important to acknowledge positive traits in others?

WHAT'S YOUR OPINION?

NAME:

DIVERSITY PURSUIT

CELEBRATE DIFFERENCES!

Has a family member with a disability	Has learned about diversity before	Speaks more than one language	Listens to the same type of music I do	Celebrates Kwanzaa
Has more than one race or culture in his/her family	Has read a book about a group of people different from himself/herself	Has assisted someone with a disability	Has more than two sisters	Wears clothing unique to his/her culture
Has a close friend of the opposite gender	Has a name with religious or cultural significance	Has ever been treated differently because of the way he/she looks	Likes Italian food	Has traveled to another country
Is an only child	Celebrates holidays that are different from mine	Writes to or e-mails someone in another country	Went to a religious school	Was born in another country
Has experienced prejudice	Has attended a cultural heritage parade or celebration	Has participated in a Big Brother or Big Sister program	Knows sign language	Does his/her homework

Leadership Skills :: High School Workbook

NAME: _____

QUESTIONS

1. Did anything surprise you during the Diversity Pursuit game? What was it?

2. Choose one square on the Diversity Pursuit worksheet that you would like to talk about further. Find the person who signed it, and ask them about what they wrote.

NAME:

QUESTIONS

1. How did your group do in carrying out the plan on your music video?

2. What did you observe about yourself within the group dynamic?

3. How did your participation benefit the group?

4. What are some ways that you cooperate with others at home? In school? At work? With your friends?

NAME:

DIG IN

WHAT'S YOUR OPINION?

How can you find the balance between following through on a plan and responding to what comes up in the moment?

PAPER CLIP CHAIN DIRECTIONS

As a group, make a paper clip chain in the following sequence:

1. 5 blue clips
2. 5 pink clips
3. 5 green clips
4. 5 black clips
5. 5 yellow clips

There are twenty-five paper clips of various colors in your container.

When your group has completed the chain in the sequence above, have one member of the group place the chain around his/her neck and come to the front of the room.

You have ten minutes to complete this task.

NAME: _____

QUESTIONS

WHAT DO YOU THINK?

What are some ways that you've helped others to solve problems?

NAME:

DIG IN

1. When was a time you thought outside the box to solve a problem?

2. How did it go?

3. When could you do this in the future?

WHAT'S YOUR OPINION?

NAME:

QUESTIONS

WHAT DO YOU THINK?

What was it like creating an original story as a group?

NAME:

DIG IN

1. What's the value of working in a group for an activity like creating a story?

2. What did you discover about your creative self?

WHAT'S YOUR OPINION?

4
Vision and Imagination

NAME:

BIOGRAPHY OF A STRANGER

Choose **one** person in the photograph and answer the questions below about that person. Be specific!

1. Who is this person? (Include name, age, and occupation.)

2. Where is he/she?

3. Why is he/she there?

4. Where does this person want to be in five years?

5. How does this person spend his/her day?

6. What does he/she want other people to think about him/her?

7. What is this person's greatest fear?

8. What does this person dream of doing in his/her life?

9. What does this person care about the most?

NAME:

THREE LINES AND A SECRET

Write three additional lines that your character might say:

To himself/herself

To a friend or family member

To a stranger

Brainstorm possible secrets that your character might have, and write down one that he/she has never told to anyone.

NAME: _____

DIG DEEPER

You are now going to dig deeper into the thoughts of the character you created in Biography of a Stranger. What is an important image in the photo your teacher has given you? Describe that image in the blank below to give the reader an idea of how your character sometimes feels. (For example, if you see an image of a tree on the top of a mountain, you could write, "Sometimes I feel like a tree on the top of a mountain.")

Sometimes I feel like a

When I feel this way the world becomes a

A CLOSER LOOK...

STEPPIN' UP RULES

1. Each group receives a deck of cards that remains facedown in the middle of the table.

2. The dealer gives each player five cards from the deck. Players may look at their cards.

3. The goal of the game is to get a hand of five cards that includes one Goal card and four Step cards that can lead to achieving that goal.

4. The dealer turns one card from the deck faceup. This is the discard pile.

5. The player to the dealer's right starts. He/she must pick a card from either the deck at the center of the table (the cards that are facedown) or from the discard pile next to the deck (the cards that are faceup). Then he/she must discard one card from his/her deck onto the discard pile. Every player must pick one card and discard one card each turn.

6. This continues until one person in the group raises his/her hand to signal that he/she has four Step cards that lead to a Goal card.

NAME:

STEPPIN' UP MY FUTURE

My goal ten years from now is:

START WITH ONE STEP...

The steps I can take to achieve my goal are:

NAME: _____

YOUR PLAN OF ACTION

Complete the table below by filling in each of your personal goals for the year, the obstacles or conflicts that might get in the way of each goal, initiatives you can take to overcome those obstacles, and dates you want to set for accomplishing your initiatives.

GOALS	OBSTACLES / CONFLICT	INITIATIVES	DATE TO ACCOMPLISH
Example: Graduate high school	Lack of studying Partying Fighting	Find a study partner Party only on weekends See my counselor to help me stop fighting in school	September Immediately Monday

NAME: _____

TRIBUTE TO YOU

Writing goals can be hard. Start by dreaming big about your future self.

Imagine that you are going to be honored as an outstanding leader at a gala. All of your friends and family are gathering to celebrate your contributions. Several people will make speeches about you. What would you like them to say? What sorts of words, phrases, and images might they use to describe you?

5

Conflict Management

NAME:

ROLE PLAY SETUP

Who are your characters?

Character 1

Name:

Age:

Occupation:

Favorite activity:

Character 2

Name:

Age:

Occupation:

Favorite activity:

Do the characters know each other? If so, what is their relationship?

What is the conflict in the scene?

Where does the scene take place?

NAME:

DIALOGUE WRITING

Scene title:

Character 1:

Character 2:

1:

2:

1:

2:

1:

2:

1:

2:

1:

2:

NAME: _____

QUESTIONS

1. How was the character you played different or similar to the character from Biography of a Stranger?

2. What was it like for you to share your role play in front of the class?

NAME:

DIG IN

1. When are other times in life when it could be useful to be able to get up in front of a group?

2. How could being able to speak in front of a group benefit you?

WHAT'S YOUR OPINION?

NAME:

CONFLICT DETECTIVE

Think about your life and write a report about a conflict that you were a part of or that you witnessed. Choose from one of these three categories and describe what happened or what you saw.

1. Inner conflict—something you were confused about inside yourself

2. Conflict between you and someone else

3. A conflict you saw involving other people, either in real life or on TV/in a movie

Conflict Category:

Description of Conflict:

NAME: _____

QUESTIONS

WHAT DO YOU THINK?

1. What surprised you about the conflict you wrote about?

2. What is healthy conflict to you?

3. What is unhealthy conflict?

NAME:

DIG IN

1. What type of conflict is the most challenging for you?

2. Why?

WHAT'S YOUR OPINION?

ARE YOU AN EFFECTIVE COMMUNICATOR?

- ❏ Do you make eye contact?
- ❏ Do you watch other people's body postures and facial expressions?
- ❏ Do you empathize and try to understand people's feelings, thoughts, and actions?
- ❏ Do you keep yourself from interrupting and let the other person finish, even if you think that you already know what he/she means?
- ❏ Do you ask questions to clarify information?
- ❏ Do you smile and nod your head to show interest?
- ❏ Do you listen even if you do not like the person who is talking or what the person is saying?
- ❏ Do you ignore outside distractions?
- ❏ Do you listen for and remember important points?
- ❏ Do you keep yourself from judging what is being said? Do you remain neutral?

Communication Pitfalls

In addition to using closed questions or statements, here are some surefire ways to shut down communication:

- ❏ Interrupt
- ❏ Laugh or ridicule
- ❏ Offer advice
- ❏ Criticize
- ❏ Judge
- ❏ Bring up your own experience

Be sure to avoid these common pitfalls!

ACTIVE LISTENING VOCABULARY

Communication: When the receiver gets the message that the sender intends.

Conflict: 1) A struggle between opposing forces. 2) A condition of opposition and discord involving ideas, interests, etcetera. 3) A clash between contradictory impulses within an individual.

Attending: Using nonverbal behaviors to show that you hear and understand. "Nonverbal" means you do not talk. Nonverbal behaviors include:

- Eye contact
- Facial expressions
- Posture
- Gestures
- Encouraging sounds

If you are leaning forward, smiling, nodding, and ignoring outside distractions, then you are attending.

Summarizing: 1) Restating facts by repeating the most important points and getting rid of extra information. 2) Reflecting feelings about the conflict. (You become a mirror for the conflict. It is very important when summarizing to recognize feelings as well as facts.)

Clarifying: Using open-ended questions or statements to get additional information and to make sure that you understand the speaker.

NAME:

ARE YOU LISTENING?

Describe a situation in which you used active listening.

What attending skills did you use to show that you were listening?

Describe how it felt to really listen to someone and how that person responded to your attentiveness.

NAME: _____

QUESTIONS

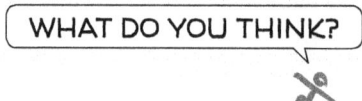

1. During the warm-up, in which you planned a school dance, what did you think was the least productive communication behavior?

2. What's the hardest part of listening for you? Is it attending, summarizing, or clarifying?

NAME:

DIG IN

1. What types of communicators do you see around you?

2. Who is someone in your life who you think is a great communicator?

3. What does that person do to make you feel that way?

WHAT'S YOUR OPINION?

ACTIVE LISTENING MONOLOGUE

Little Red Riding Hood

I'm Red Riding Hood. They used to call me Little Red Riding Hood, but they don't anymore. The Wolf and I have had this problem for a long time. You see, I was taking a loaf of fresh bread and some cakes to my granny's cottage on the other side of the woods. Granny wasn't well, so I thought I would pick some flowers for her along the way.

I was picking the flowers when the Wolf jumped out from behind a tree and started asking me a bunch of questions. He wanted to know what I was doing and where I was going, and he kept grinning this wicked grin and smacking his lips together.

He was being so gross and rude. Then he ran away. I feel like a young lady can't even walk in the woods these days without being harassed.

The Wolf

I am the Wolf. The forest is my home. I care about it and try to keep it clean. One day, when I was cleaning up the garbage that some people had left behind, I heard footsteps. I leapt behind a tree and saw a girl coming down the trail carrying a basket.

I was suspicious because she was dressed in this strange red cape, and her head was covered up as if she didn't want anyone to know who she was. She started picking my flowers and stepping on my new little pine trees.

Naturally, I stopped to ask her what she was doing and all that. She gave me this song and dance about going to her granny's house with a basket of goodies. I know this girl's granny. I thought we should teach Red Riding Hood a lesson for prancing on my pine trees and picking my flowers in that getup. I let her go on her way, but I ran ahead to her granny's cottage.

When I saw Granny, I explained what had happened, and she agreed that her granddaughter needed to learn a lesson. Granny hid under the bed, and I dressed up in her nightgown.

NAME: _____

ARE YOU REALLY LISTENING?

Think of a conflict that you have had that was resolved because you **really** listened to the other person.

Describe the conflict.

How was listening important in resolving this conflict?

What might have happened in this conflict if you had not used your active-listening skills?

NAME: _____

TRANSLATION SHEET

Translate this: You always get our class into trouble. You never stop talking, even when the teacher asks you to be quiet.

To this:

I feel .... because ....

I would like ....
....
....

Translate this: You always want it your way when we're picking movies. When you don't get your way, you start fighting with everyone.

To this:

I feel .... because ....

I would like ....
....
....

Leadership Skills :: High School Workbook

Translate this: You always borrow my stuff and never give it back.

To this:

I feel . . . . because . . . .

I would like . . . .
. . . .
. . . .
. . . .

Translate this: You always say bad things about people. You hurt everyone's feelings, and no one wants to be your friend.

To this:

I feel . . . . because . . . .

I would like . . . .
. . . .
. . . .
. . . .

Translate this: You always make fun of me when I don't know the answer to the question. It makes me feel dumb! You're the stupid one!

To this:

I feel . . . . because . . . .

I would like . . . .
. . . .
. . . .
. . . .

NAME:

"I" MESSAGES IN REAL LIFE

Try using an "I" message in a real-life conflict situation. Write about it by answering the questions below.

1. What was your conflict?

2. With whom did you have this conflict?

3. What "I" message did you use?

4. What was this person's response?

5. How did it feel?

6. What do you think would have happened if you had used a "You" message instead?

TELL ME HOW YOU FEEL!

NAME: _____

RESPONSES TO ANGER

1. Under the Response to Anger heading below, list ten ways that people respond to anger. Examples: listening to music, hitting something, eating.

2. After listing possible responses, decide whether each response is healthy, unhealthy, or both. Place a check mark in the appropriate space.

Use these definitions as your guidelines for healthy and unhealthy responses to anger:

- A healthy response to anger is dealing with the situation without harming yourself or others.

- An unhealthy response to anger is dealing with the situation by intentionally or unintentionally doing harm to yourself or others.

RESPONSE TO ANGER	HEALTHY	UNHEALTHY	BOTH

RESPONSE TO ANGER	HEALTHY	UNHEALTHY	BOTH

DON'T FORGET TO BREATHE!

LEARNING THE ABCS OF ANGER

A = The Anger Trigger

Whatever has triggered the response of anger.

Examples of Anger Triggers:
1. Your mom won't let you stay out late on a school night.
2. Your little brother borrows your clothes without asking.
3. Your friend lies to you.

B = The Behavior Response

What you do when you get angry.

Examples of Behavior Responses:
1. You yell at your mom.
2. You tell your brother that you are angry at him for disrespecting you and that if he doesn't ask for your permission before borrowing your clothes, you won't let him borrow anything anymore.
3. You curse at your friend.

C = The Consequence

The consequence of controlling or not controlling your anger.

Examples of Consequences:
1. Your mother grounds you for yelling at her.
2. Next time, your brother asks to borrow clothes before taking them.
3. You get into a fight at school and are expelled.

NAME: _____

THE ABCS OF ANGER WORKSHEET

A. **THE ANGER TRIGGER** WHAT ARE THREE THINGS THAT MAKE YOU ANGRY?	B. **THE BEHAVIOR RESPONSE** HOW DO YOU REACT?	C. **THE CONSEQUENCE** WHAT IS THE RESULT OF YOUR BEHAVIOR?
EXAMPLE: MY FRIEND LIES TO ME.	I CURSE AT HIM.	I GET IN A FIGHT AT SCHOOL, AND I AM EXPELLED.

Leadership Skills :: High School Workbook

NAME:

TAKE MY ADVICE

Dear . . . . ,

I get so mad when kids at school make fun of me. I feel like I want to get in a fight, but I know that that is not the best thing to do. How can I deal with my anger in a better way?

Sincerely,

Always in Trouble

IF I WERE YOU …

Dear Always in Trouble,

NAME:

DIG IN

1. What is a situation that might make you angry?

2. What is a healthy way that you could respond when you feel angry?

WHAT'S YOUR OPINION?

NAME:

ROLE PLAY SETUP

Who are your characters?

Character 1

Name:

Age:

Occupation:

Favorite activity:

Character 2

Name:

Age:

Occupation:

Favorite activity:

Do the characters know each other? If so, what is their relationship?

What is the conflict in the scene?

Where does the scene take place?

GIVIN' IT CHECKLIST

Skill: Giving Negative Feedback

1. Stay calm and ask if you can talk to the person.

2. Say something positive.

3. Tell the person what's on your mind, using the "I" message format (I feel .... because ....).

4. Ask if the person understands.

5. Ask for change (I would like ....). or: Ask how the person feels about it.

6. Thank the person for listening.

IF YOU WANT SOMEONE TO HEAR YOU ...

NAME:

DIALOGUE WRITING

Scene title:

Character 1:

Character 2:

1:

2:

1:

2:

1:

2:

1:

2:

1:

2:

NAME:

QUESTIONS

WHAT DO YOU THINK?

What is a strategy we haven't discussed that could resolve the conflict in your scene? Think outside the box!

NAME: _____

DIG IN

1. Where in your life could this skill of **Givin' It** be useful?

2. How does this relate to your leadership style?

WHAT'S YOUR OPINION?

NAME:

ROLE PLAY SETUP

Who are your characters?

Character 1

Name:

Age:

Occupation:

Favorite activity:

Character 2

Name:

Age:

Occupation:

Favorite activity:

Do the characters know each other? If so, what is their relationship?

What is the conflict in the scene?

Where does the scene take place?

TAKIN' IT CHECKLIST

Skill: Receiving Negative Feedback

1. Stay calm and listen to what the other person has to say. Do not interrupt him/her.

2. Once he/she has finished talking, ask him/her to explain anything you don't understand.

3. Tell the person you understand, and paraphrase what he/she has said.

4. Agree and apologize.
   or: Ask if you can tell your point of view.

5. Ask what the person wants you to do.

WHEN IT'S YOUR TURN TO LISTEN...

NAME:

DIALOGUE WRITING

Scene title:

Character 1:

Character 2:

1:

2:

1:

2:

1:

2:

1:

2:

1:

2:

NAME: _____

DIG IN

1. When is a time that you might need to hear negative feedback?

2. How could you benefit from negative feedback?

3. When have you received negative feedback and turned it into something positive?

WHAT'S YOUR OPINION?

NAME:

TO BLANK OR NOT TO BLANK

KEEP TRACK!

1. Write down all of the decisions that you made today in the space below. Then write down the consequences of those decisions.

2. In the first column, put an X by the decisions that you really thought through and an O by the decisions that you made out of habit or without thinking.

3. Put an asterisk (*) by the decisions that had positive consequences.

X OR O?	DECISION	CONSEQUENCE

LEADERSHIP SKILLS :: HIGH SCHOOL WORKBOOK 79

NAME:

C.D.C. — SETTING THE SCENE

Who are your characters?

Character 1

Name:

Age:

Occupation:

Favorite thing to do:

Character 2

Name:

Age:

Occupation:

Favorite thing to do:

Do the characters know each other? If so, what is the relationship?

Where does the scene take place?

What is the situation?

NAME:

QUESTIONS

WHAT DO YOU THINK?

1. Is there any relationship between thinking through or not thinking through a decision and the resulting consequences? If yes, why do you think so?

2. Did your attitude, values, or goals have anything to do with whether or not a decision received an **X** or an **O**?

3. What can you do to make more decisions that might have positive consequences?

NAME:

CHOICES, DECISIONS, CONSEQUENCES ROLE PLAY

1. Decide what the situation is.

2. Decide who the characters will be.

3. Decide where the scene will take place.

4. List all of the possible choices, decisions, and consequences in the table on the following page.

5. Select one decision to be enacted and circle it.

6. Select one consequence to be enacted and circle it.

7. Decide who will play character A and character B in the scene.
   Only two people should be acting in the scene. The others in the group may introduce the scene, direct it, freeze it, etcetera.

8. Rehearse the scene.

Situation:

DECISIONS, DECISIONS!

Character A:

Character B:

Where will the scene take place?

CHOICES	DECISIONS	CONSEQUENCES

NAME:

DECISIONS

Select a real-life situation in which you have to make an important decision. Complete the **Choices, Decisions, Consequences** chart below.

Situation:

CHOICES	DECISIONS	CONSEQUENCES

NAME:

QUESTIONS

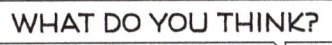  

1. What was the personal dilemma you described in class?

2. What were the steps you took to solve it?

NAME:

DIG IN

"Problems are not stop signs, they are guidelines."

—Robert H. Schuller

What does this quote mean to you?

WHAT'S YOUR OPINION?

CONFLICT MANAGEMENT

- Conflict is a part of life.

- A conflict is a problem to be solved.

- There is more than one way to solve a problem.

- Sometimes we can solve problems so that everybody wins.

- Everybody can learn to be a problem solver.

- Feelings are important. Unless feelings are heard and listened to, it is very difficult to solve a problem.

- It is okay to get help when solving a conflict.

- Conflict involves choices, decisions, and consequences.

- Sometimes a conflict cannot be solved all at once. Take one step at a time.

- There are skills to learn to solve conflicts. Through practice we can improve our skills for solving conflicts creatively.

NAME:

CONFLICT STATUES

Add your drawing from Conflict Statues here.

6
Social Responsibility

NAME:

QUESTIONS

1. What happened in your group?

2. How did you decide which problem to address?

3. What can you do in your life to help create a better world?

NAME:

ACTION PLAN

IT'S ALL IN THE DETAILS!

1. The Need:

2. Brainstorm list of ways to address the need:

3. Assign roles:

NAME	JOB/TASK	WHY THIS PERSON FOR THE JOB?

4. Plan of Action/Checklist:

ACTION	PEOPLE INVOLVED	DEADLINE	COMPLETED
STEP 1:			
STEP 2:			
STEP 3:			
STEP 4:			
STEP 5:			
STEP 6:			

ACTION PLAN EXAMPLE

TAKE A LOOK!

1. The Need: **Fire**
2. Brainstorm list of ways to address the need:
   - Rub sticks together
   - Use a mirror or glasses to reflect sun
   - Find matches or lighter
   - Build hole in ground
3. Assign roles:

NAME	JOB/TASK	WHY THIS PERSON FOR THE JOB?
JOHN	COLLECT STONES	HE CAN CARRY LOTS OF WEIGHT.
SERENA	COLLECT STICKS	SHE WANTS TO.
JOSE	DIG HOLE IN SAND	HE CAN USE HIS BASEBALL CAP TO SCOOP SAND.
MARCUS & JENNY	CUT WOOD	THEY KNOW HOW TO USE A SAW.
TINA	CREATE FLAME	SHE CAN REFLECT THE SUN WITH HER GLASSES.

4. Plan of Action/Checklist:

ACTION	PEOPLE INVOLVED	DEADLINE	COMPLETED
STEP 1: **FIND LOCATION FOR FIRE PIT**	EVERYONE	TODAY, NOON	X
STEP 2: **DIG HOLE IN SAND**	JOSE	TODAY, 2:00 PM	
STEP 3: **COLLECT STONES TO PUT AROUND PIT**	JOHN	TODAY, 3:00 PM	X
STEP 4: **CUT WOOD FROM BAMBOO TREES**	MARCUS & JENNY	TODAY, 4:00 PM	
STEP 5: **COLLECT STICKS**	SERENA	TODAY, 4:00 PM	
STEP 6: **LIGHT FIRE**	TINA	TODAY, 5:00 PM	

TRIBE SURVIVAL MISSION

The Need: **Shelter**

Your tribe is responsible for solving the shelter problem on the island. A storm is due in tonight, so it is very important that shelter is created for everyone on the island (twenty-five people). The map will provide you with information about the natural materials available to you (e.g., trees). Your tribe has only the following tools: one saw and four boxes of nails (approximately one hundred nails per box).

Remember that you must make enough shelter for twenty-five people. It can be one big place or several smaller ones.

Fill out the **Action Plan** worksheet and draw a picture of your plans to present to the other tribes.

The Need: **Food**

Your tribe is responsible for providing food for everyone on the island (twenty-five people) for dinner tonight. The map will provide you with information about the natural materials available to you (e.g., fruit). Your tribe has only the following tool: one pocketknife. A fire will be available if needed.

Fill out the **Action Plan** worksheet and prepare a menu of tonight's dinner to present to the other tribes. Include a brief explanation of how you will get each food.

The Need: **Water**

Your tribe is responsible for providing drinking water for all the people on the island (twenty-five people). The rations have run out and water must be obtained by nightfall. The map will provide you with information about the natural materials available to you. There is only one natural freshwater spring.

Right now there is no mode of transportation to get to the spring and no container to bring the water back to the camp. Your tribe has only the following tools: one pocketknife and one saw.

Fill out the **Action Plan** worksheet and prepare a short presentation for the other tribes on how you will get water back to camp.

The Need: **Entertainment**

Your tribe is responsible for providing tonight's entertainment on the island. Everyone has been working very hard and needs to have some fun. Plan an entertainment event for the twenty-five people on the island. The map will provide you with information about the natural materials available to you. Remember: there are no radios or electronic items on the island.

Fill out the **Action Plan** worksheet and prepare to present your idea to the other tribes.

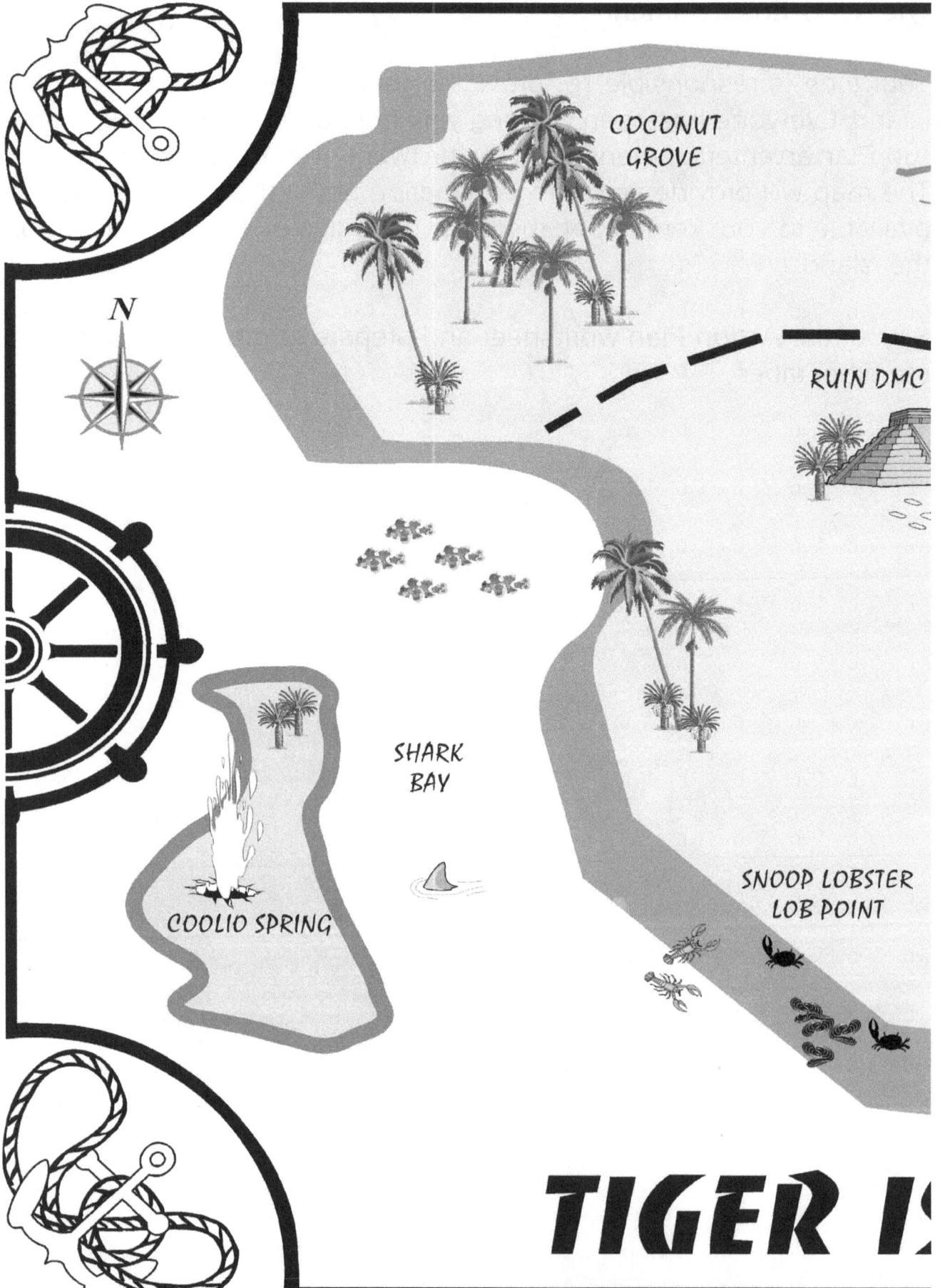

ORGANIZATIONAL MODEL

1. Identify or assess a need or problem.

2. Brainstorm ways to address the need or problem.

3. Assign roles.

4. Create a specific plan of action.

5. Execute the plan.

6. Assess individual and group achievement/participation.

Note: Steps 3 and 4 may be reversed if necessary.

NAME:

QUESTIONS

 WHAT DO YOU THINK?

What came up for you when you developed the organizational model in your tribe?

NAME: _____

DIG IN

1. What tribes are you a part of in your life?

2. What are some ways that your tribe can support you in one of your goals?

3. In the closing in class, were there any ideas for how to use the organizational model that stood out to you? Why?

WHAT'S YOUR OPINION?

7

Project Work

NAME:

WHO AM I? PROJECT GUIDE

Step 1: Brainstorm interview questions.

Step 2: Copy questions and possible projects from the class chart into chart below.

Step 3: Choose the project you want to do.

Step 4: Make a list of materials you will need.

Step 5: Make a To-Do List of what you will need to do to complete your project.

IMAGINE YOUR LIFE...

Step 2: Questions

WHO AM I? QUESTIONS	CREATIVE PROJECTS THAT ANSWER THE QUESTIONS
EXAMPLE: "WHAT MOMENT OF YOUR LIFE WOULD YOU LIKE TO LIVE OVER AGAIN AND WHY?"	EXAMPLE: WRITE AN ESSAY, MONOLOGUE, OR POEM ABOUT THAT MOMENT. MAKE A PAINTING OR COLLAGE ABOUT THAT MOMENT.

Step 3: Choose

What question will my project answer?

My project is:

Step 4: Materials

What materials will I need to complete my project?

Step 5: To-Do List

What will I need to do to complete my project?

NAME:

QUESTIONS

1. What was exciting about doing this project?

2. What was scary?

3. What surprised you the most about what your classmates shared through their projects?

NAME: _____

DIG IN

1. Why is it important to take the time to think about the question "Who Am I?"

2. How does this relate to your personal leadership style?

WHAT'S YOUR OPINION?

NAME: _____

WHO AM I? REFLECTION

How has your behavior in Leadership class changed since the beginning of the program?

Describe your **Who Am I?** project. What made you choose your question? How did you figure out how to answer the question in a creative way?

What advice would you give to a student who is starting this course next year?

What advice would you give to the Leadership Program on how to improve the class?

YOU'RE ON YOUR WAY!

NAME:

DIG IN

"Finding your voice is about engaging with the world."

—Phil Slater

What does this quote mean to you?

WHAT'S YOUR OPINION?

Other program curriculum support available from The Leadership Program at www.tlpnyc.com/leadership-marketplace.

Boys 2 MENtors: Curriculum Manual

Boys 2 MENtors: Student Workbook

Empowering Upstanders: A School-Based Bullying Prevention Program

Empowering Upstanders: Student Workbook

HERstory: Curriculum Suite

HERstory: Student Writing Companion

Leadership Skills: High School Manual: Violence Prevention Project

Leadership Skills: Middle School Workbook: Violence Prevention Project

Leadership Skills: Middle School Manual: Violence Prevention Project

www.ingramcontent.com/pod-product-compliance
Lightning Source LLC
Chambersburg PA
CBHW081841170426
43199CB00017B/2803